RIFLE
SHOOTING

BOY SCOUTS OF AMERICA
IRVING, TEXAS

**1995 Printing of the
1990 Revision**

Requirements

1. Do the following:

   a. Explain why BB and pellet air guns must always be treated with the same respect as firearms.

   b. Describe how you would react if a friend visiting your home asked to see your or your family's firearm(s).

   c. Explain the need, use, and types of eye and ear protection.

   d. Give the main points of the laws for owning and using guns in your community and state.

   e. Explain how hunting is related to the wise use of renewable wildlife resources.

   f. Explain the main points of hunting laws in your state and give any special laws on the use of guns or ammunition.

   g. List the kinds of wildlife that can be legally hunted in your state.

   h. Identify and explain the rifle sports shot in the Olympic Games. Identify places in your community where you could shoot these sports.

   i. List the sources that you could contact for information on firearms and their use.

2. Do ONE of the following options:

   Option A—Rifle Shooting
   (Modern Cartridge Type)

   a. Identify the principal parts of a rifle, action types, and how they function.

   b. Identify and demonstrate the three rules for handling a rifle safely.

Copyright 1989
Boy Scouts of America
Irving, Texas
ISBN 0-8395-3330-6
No. 33330   Printed in U.S.A.   25M1095

c. Identify rifle ammunition parts and their function.

d. Identify seven different calibers of rifle ammunition. Explain which one you would use and why.

e. Identify and demonstrate the five fundamentals of shooting a rifle.

f. Identify and explain each rule for shooting a rifle safely.

g. Demonstrate the knowledge, skill, and attitude necessary to safely shoot a target from the bench rest position, using the five fundamentals of rifle shooting.

h. Identify the materials needed to clean a rifle.

i. Demonstrate how to clean a rifle safely.

j. Demonstrate the standing, kneeling, prone, and sitting positions.

k. Discuss what points you would consider in selecting a rifle.

l. Using a .22 caliber rimfire rifle and shooting from a bench rest (supported) position at 50 feet, fire five groups (three shots per group) that can be covered by a quarter. Adjust sights to center the group on the target and fire five groups (five shots per group). According to the target used, each shot in the group must meet the following minimum score: (1) A-32 targets—9, (2) A-17 or TQ-1 targets—8, (3) A-36 targets—6.

Option B—Air Rifle Shooting
(BB or Pellet)

a. Identify the principal parts of an air rifle, action types, and how they function.

b. Identify and demonstrate the three rules for handling a rifle safely.

c. Identify various types of air rifle ammunition.

d. Identify different calibers of air rifle ammunition.

e. Identify and demonstrate the five fundamentals of shooting a rifle.

f. Identify and explain each rule for shooting an air rifle safely.

g. Demonstrate the knowledge, skill, and attitude necessary to safely shoot a target from the bench rest position, using the five fundamentals of rifle shooting.

h. Identify the materials needed to clean an air rifle.

i. Demonstrate how to clean an air rifle safely.

j. Demonstrate the standing, kneeling, prone, and sitting positions.

k. Discuss what points you would consider in selecting an air rifle.

l. Using a BB or pellet air rifle and shooting from a bench rest (supported) position, fire five groups (three shots per group) that can be covered by a quarter. Adjust sights to center the group on the target and fire five groups (five shots per group). According to the target used, each shot in the group must meet the following minimum score: (1) BB rifle at 15 feet or 5 meters using TQ-5 targets—8; (2) pellet air rifle at 25 feet using TQ-5 target—8, at 33 feet or 10 meters using AR-1 targets—6.

Option C—Muzzle-loading Rifle Shooting

a. Discuss a brief history of the development of muzzle-loading rifles.

b. Identify principal parts of percussion and flintlock rifles and discuss how they function.

c. Demonstrate and discuss the safe handling rules of muzzle-loading rifles.

d. Identify the various grades of black powder and their proper use.

e. Discuss proper safety procedures pertaining to black powder use and storage.

f. Discuss proper components of a load.

g. Identify proper procedures and accessories used for loading a muzzle-loading rifle.

h. Demonstrate the knowledge, skill, and attitude necessary to safely shoot a muzzle-loading rifle on a range, including range procedure.

i. Shoot a target with a muzzle-loading rifle using the five fundamentals of firing the shot.

j. Identify the materials needed to clean a muzzle-loading rifle safely.

k. Demonstrate how to clean a muzzle-loading rifle safely.

l. Identify the causes of a muzzle-loading rifle's failing to fire and explain or demonstrate proper correction procedures.

m. Discuss what points you would consider in selecting a muzzle-loading rifle.

n. Using a muzzle-loading rifle of any caliber and shooting from a bench rest (supported) position, fire three groups (three shots per group) that can be covered by the base of a standard-size soft drink can. Center the group on the target and fire three groups (five shots per group). According to the target used, each shot in the group must meet the following minimum score: (1) at 25 yards using NRA A-23 or NMLRA 50-yard targets—8; (2) at 50 yards using NRA A-25 or NMLRA 100-yard targets—8.

Contents

Rifle Parts

Your rifle is a precision instrument, designed for precise work. It is designed to shoot a bullet to hit where the barrel is pointed.

It will be helpful to learn the parts of your rifle. Then, when you read about how to handle your gun, you'll be able to quickly absorb the information.

Your rifle is divided into three major parts.

The stock—the handle by which the rifle is held

The barrel—the metal tube through which the bullet passes when the rifle is fired

The action—the section of the rifle containing the moving parts that load, fire, and unload the rifle

Let's look at each of these major parts.

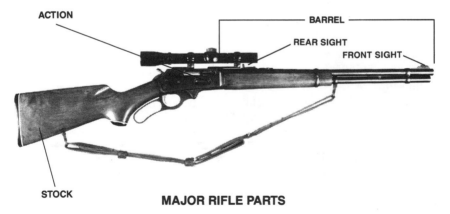

MAJOR RIFLE PARTS

The Stock

Most stocks are made of selected wood, but today more and more stocks are made of fiberglass or other synthetic materials. The stock has special design features to give the shooter comfort, ease of handling, and maximum shooting accuracy. The stock is divided into four parts: butt, comb, grip, and fore-end.

RIFLE PARTS

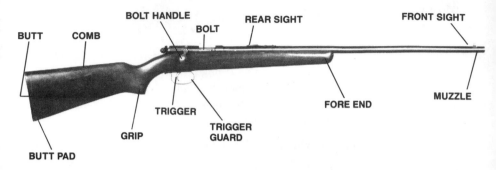

The butt is the rear portion of the stock. It is usually contoured to fit comfortably against the shoulder. The comb is the top portion of the stock upon which the shooter rests his cheek. The grip, or "small of the stock," is the area where the hand grasps the stock when squeezing the trigger. The fore-end is the part of the stock that extends under the barrel. This is the area where your other hand holds the rifle to support it.

The Barrel

The hollow inside the barrel—the hole through which the bullet passes—is called the bore. The bore is measured in hundredths or thousandths of an inch or in millimeters. This measurement is called the caliber of the rifle. The wider the diameter of the bore, the larger the caliber, and, therefore, the larger the size of bullet it will take. The opening through which the bullet leaves the barrel is called the muzzle. The rear of the barrel is called the

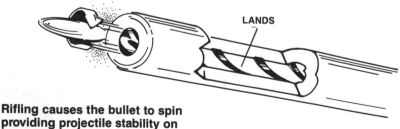

Rifling causes the bullet to spin providing projectile stability on its flight to the target.

breech. The chamber is located at the breech end of the barrel. That is the portion of the bore into which one round of ammunition (cartridge) is placed for firing. Chambers are shaped identically to the ammunition. As long as you are using the proper size ammunition, the fit should be nearly perfect.

For the remaining length of the barrel, the bore is lined with a series of spiral grooves, quite like the grooves on the inside of a machine nut. The flat, raised ridges of metal standing between the grooves are called "lands." When a bullet passes through the barrel, the lands cut into the bullet to make it spin. This spinning action makes the bullet more stable and accurate in its flight toward the target. The bullet in flight is similar to a well-thrown football. The grooves and lands inside the barrel are known as rifling, which is how the rifle got its name.

The Action

The action allows the shooter to load, shoot, and unload the rifle. There are several different designs or types of actions to do this job. These include bolt, lever, pump, hinge, and semiautomatic actions.

Loading is achieved by first opening the action. This allows you to place a cartridge in the chamber. With the cartridge in place, the action is then closed. In most rifles, opening and closing the action cocks the firing pin, making the rifle ready to be fired. Some rifles must be cocked separately. Firing takes place when you squeeze the trigger. This allows the firing pin to be driven forward.

When you open the action after firing, the used cartridge is usually ejected so that a new one can be loaded.

Many rifle actions have two other features— the magazine and the safety.

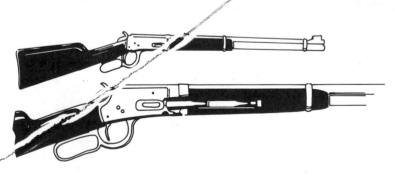

Tube magazine

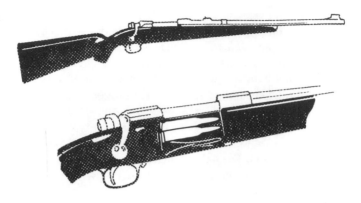

Box magazine

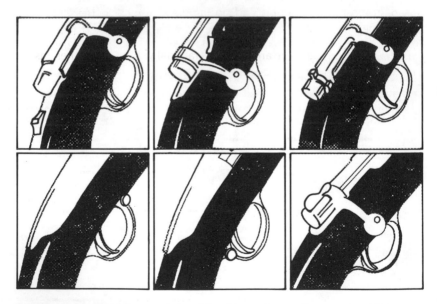

Safeties are found in a variety of locations depending on the rifle's manufacture and design.

The magazine is a container into which several cartridges can be placed. The two most common types of magazines are a box type located inside the bottom portion of the action, and a tube type located under the barrel, or in the stock. There are also separate magazines or clips that can be loaded and then slipped into place in the gun.

No rifle chamber can contain more than one cartridge at a time; the magazine makes it possible to load a new cartridge into the chamber without having to load it by hand. When the action is opened and closed, a new cartridge is pushed from the magazine into the chamber. The rifle can then be fired each time the trigger is pulled until the magazine is empty.

The safety is a mechanical device. When the safety is in the "on" position, it should block the operation of the trigger, thus preventing the rifle from firing. Remember, the safety is mechanical, and subject to malfunction. Never depend on it as a replacement for following the safety rules. Because of the false sense of security safeties can create ("I thought the safety was on"), they may have contributed to more mishaps than they have prevented. Get the point—*you* are the safety!

Types of Actions

There are six popular types of cartridge rifle actions. To give a general idea of how these actions operate, the following list describes the loading and unloading procedures for some of the more common rifle designs. It should be noted that there are many operational variations for these as well as other types of action designs. You must thoroughly study and understand your rifle's operation manual before using your rifle.

Bolt. The bolt action rifle operates on a lift, pull, and push sequence similar to a door bolt. The bolt action is probably the most common type of action. Many feel it is the strongest, most accurate of the action types.

Bolt action rifle

Pump. On pump, or slide action rifles, the forearm of the stock is pumped back and forth to open and close the action. Experienced marksmen, using a pump action rifle, can quickly load, fire, and eject the spent cartridge while keeping the rifle pointed toward the target.

Lever. The action on a lever action rifle is opened by pulling the cocking lever downward and forward away from the stock. It is closed by simply returning the lever to its original position. Lever action rifles, like pump action rifles, also allow the rapid reloading of additional cartridges.

Semiautomatic. These actions are sometimes appropriately called repeaters or autoloaders. Each time a semiautomatic rifle is fired, burning powder in the cartridge produces gas that provides the energy to operate the action.

Hinge. The hinge action opens similarly to the movement of a door hinge. When the release lever is pushed to one side, the barrel swings downward away from the breech block. Hinge action rifles may have one, two, or three barrels. Double rifles are built either as an "over and under" or a "side by side," depending on the placement of the barrels. Three-barreled guns usually have a combination of shotgun and rifle barrels and are often called *drillings*.

Falling block. The falling block action uses a breech block instead of a bolt. The action is opened by lowering the trigger guard or the small lever under it that causes the breech block to "fall" down and away from the barrel. Raising the lever closes the action and covers the breech end of the barrel. Falling block rifles are all single-shot rifles.

Sights

Sights enable you to aim the rifle. There are many different types of sights, but generally they fall into three categories: optical, open, and aperture.

Optical sights are small telescopes mounted atop the barrel or action. They are a good sight for new shooters because they are simple to use. Optical sights have a crosshair or dot that acts as an aiming point. It's important that they be of the right design and size for the rifle. Mounting screws must be tight to ensure consistent accuracy.

Open sights are standard equipment with most factory rifles. They include an open rear sight (a notch or "V") located near the breech end of the rifle, and a front sight (a post or bead) located near the muzzle. To aim, the shooter aligns the front and rear sights and aims the aligned sights at the target.

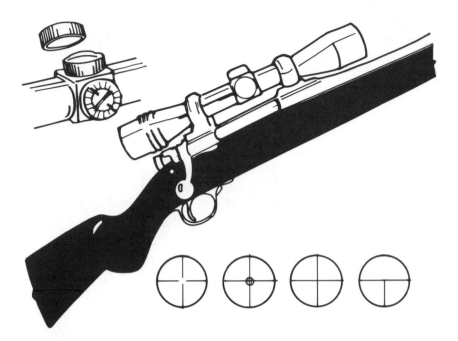

Pictured above are some of the more common reticles used in optical sights. Left to right: duplex, dot, crosshair, and post. Choice is largely a matter of personal preference. The reticle can be easily adjusted by turning the adjustment knobs on the scope in the direction you wish to move your shots on the target.

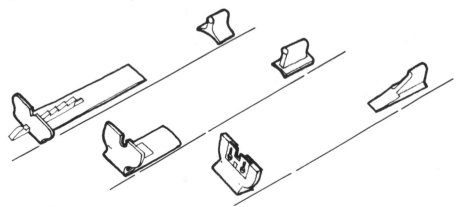

Open sights are available in a variety of adjustable and fixed designs.

Aperture sights are usually mounted on the rear of the rifle action. They are often called "peep sights" because they have a small hole in the rear sight that you look through when aiming. You simply align the front sight in the center of the rear sight opening. These sights make aligning the sights much easier and more precise than with open sights. However, they aren't as fast and easy to use as open sights when shots must be fired quickly.

Aperture rear sights, scopes, and some open sights can be precisely adjusted without special tools. This adjustment is absolutely essential because it enables you to get your shots to hit the target exactly where your sights are aimed. Usually you can make both elevation (up or down) and windage (right or left) adjustments. The rule for adjusting your sights is to move the rear sight in the same direction you want to move the location of the shot on the target.

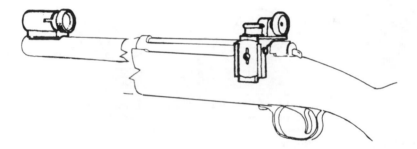

Aperture sights are popular with target shooters because they are easily adjusted.

Ammunition

To fire a rifle, you must insert ammunition into the chamber at the breech end of the barrel. The types of ammunition available today are as diverse as the rifle itself. Different sizes and shapes of ammunition have been developed to fit every sporting need. All modern rifle ammunition, however, is made up of four basic parts—the case, primer, powder, and bullet. Together they form a rifle *cartridge*.

Rifles requiring cartridges depend on burning gunpowder to produce the extremely high gas pressure that propels the bullet through the barrel and to the target.

CASES

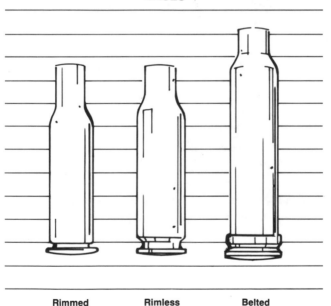

| Rimmed | Rimless | Belted |

The case is the container in which the ammunition parts are assembled. A metal, typically brass, is used in its construction. Cases come in many sizes and shapes designed to fit the matching firearm. There are two basic types— rimfire and centerfire. The difference between the two is the location of the primer.

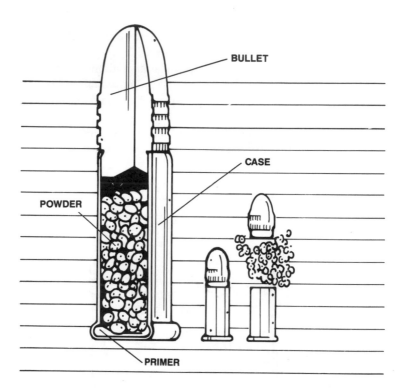

The primer is an explosive chemical mixture that detonates when hit by the firing pin. This ignites the powder charge. In rimfire ammunition (mostly .22 caliber), the priming chemical is contained inside the hollow rim at the base of the case. The rim is soft enough that when the pin strikes it a small dent is created. This indentation crushes the priming compound, causing it to detonate.

In centerfire ammunition, the primer is a separate component located in the center of the cartridge base. This type of design allows greater case strength required in high-power rifle ammunition.

The powder charge is a chemical compound designed to burn rapidly and produce a high volume of gas. When ignited by the primer, the expanding gas provides the force needed to propel the bullet.

CENTERFIRE

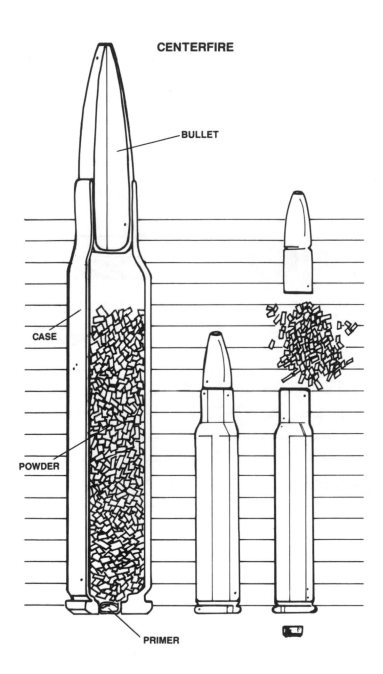

BULLET

CASE

POWDER

PRIMER

The bullet is the projectile that is shot by the rifle to the target. It is made of lead and may also have a jacket of a harder metal such as copper. The bullet must match the chamber and the bore of the rifle or an unsafe condition can result.

The diameter of the bore, measured in fractions of an inch or in millimeters, is the caliber of the gun.

Here are a few calibers and variations of bullets.

.22 short	.222 Remington	.243 Winchester	7mm Magnum
.22 long	.25-06 Remington	.270 Winchester	8mm Mauser
.22 long rifle	.30-06 Springfield	.30-30 Winchester	.300 Savage

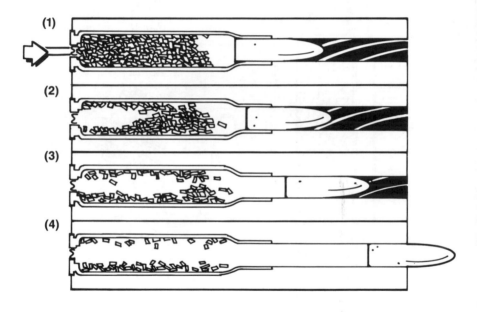

(1) Firing pin strikes primer, (2) Primer detonates igniting powder, (3) Burning powder forms gases, (4) Expanding hot gases propel bullet.

Gun Safety

When you participate in shooting sports, you're assuming a vital responsibility that affects other lives. It is vitally important to learn and practice all rifle safety rules.

When handled correctly and used properly, a rifle is not dangerous. A rifle, like any other precision machine, instrument, or piece of sports equipment, is manufactured to perform a specific task and can do so at no risk to the user or others. If a rifle is handled incorrectly or recklessly, without regard for the safety rules, then accidents can occur.

Rifle safety is a simple but ongoing process. You must first acquire a *knowledge* of how to handle rifles safely, then develop and maintain proper safe handling *skills* through practice. But the most important element to being safe is *attitude*. Safety knowledge and skills are of little value unless you have the attitude to use them all of the time. Being safe means that you are consciously keeping your gun under control. Always be alert to, and conscious of, your rifle's capabilities, and be aware of what might happen if it is used improperly.

There are basic gun safety rules that must always be applied. They fall into two major categories: the fundamental rules for safe gun handling and rules when using or storing a gun.

Fundamental Rules for Safe Rifle Handling

Three basic rules apply whenever you are handling a rifle—under any circumstances. Rule No. 1 is the "Golden Rule of Gun Safety."

1. Always keep the gun pointed in a safe direction. Whether you are shooting or simply handling your rifle, never point the muzzle at yourself or others. Common sense should dictate which

direction is safest depending on your location and other conditions. Generally, it is safest to point the rifle upward or downward.

2. Keep your finger off the trigger until you are ready to shoot. There's a natural tendency to place your finger on the trigger when picking up or

handling a rifle. Avoid it! Your finger can rest above the trigger guard along the side of the stock or better yet around the grip of the gun. Trigger guards are designed to prevent the trigger from getting bumped accidentally.

3. Keep the action open and unloaded until ready to use. Whenever you pick up or are handed any rifle, and while following rules 1 and 2, immediately open the action and visually check to see that the chamber is unloaded. If the rifle has a magazine, remove it and make sure it's empty. If you do not know how to open the rifle action, leave it alone and get help from someone who does.

Rules for Using or Storing a Gun

When you're actually engaged in shooting—whether in hunting, recreational practice, or competition—these rules must always be followed.

- **Be sure the gun is safe to operate.** Just like other tools, guns need regular maintenance to remain operable. Regular cleaning and proper storage are part of the gun's general upkeep. If there is any question concerning a gun's ability to function, a competent gunsmith should look at it.

- **Know now to safely use a gun.** Before handling a gun, learn how it operates. Know its basic parts, how to open and close the action safely, and how to safely remove any ammunition from the gun or magazine. Remember, a gun's mechanical safety device is never foolproof. Nothing can ever replace safe gun handling.

- **Use only the correct ammunition for your gun.** Only BBs, pellets, cartridges, or shells designed for a particular gun can be fired safely from that gun. Most guns have the ammunition type stamped on the barrel. Ammunition can be identified by information printed on the box and sometimes stamped on the cartridge. Do not shoot the gun if there is any question about the capability of the gun and the ammunition.

- **Know your target and what is beyond.** Be absolutely sure you have identified your target beyond any doubt. It is equally important to be aware of the area beyond your target. This means observing your prospective area of fire before you shoot. Never fire in a direction in which there are people or any other potential for mishap. Think first. Shoot second.

- **Wear ear and eye protection as appropriate.** Guns are loud and the noise can cause hearing damage. They can also emit debris and hot gas that cause eye injury. For these reasons, safety glasses and ear protection are recommended.

- **Never use alcohol or drugs before or while shooting.** Alcohol, as well as any other substance likely to impair normal mental or physical bodily functions, must not be used before or while handling or shooting guns.

- **Store guns so that they are not accessible to unauthorized persons.** Several factors should be considered when you decide on where and how you intend to store your guns. Your particular needs will be a major part of the consideration. Safe and secure storage requires that untrained individuals (especially children) be denied access to your gun.

Be aware that certain types of guns and many shooting activities require additional safety precautions.

Shooting Ranges

The supervised shooting range is one of the safest places to enjoy shooting. The operators of most ranges use standard range commands to control the shooting and to promote uniform safety practices. The purpose of range commands and rules is to let everyone shoot safely. In every case, the undisputed boss is the range officer. That person is the one giving the commands and monitoring all shooters to be sure they are complying with the safety rules. As a shooter, it's your responsibility to obey and respect him. Below are two of the standard range commands you may hear a range officer use:

1. "Commence firing."

2. "Cease firing."

No matter how formal or informal the shooting circumstances, these two commands are absolute. "Commence firing" means you may begin shooting when you are ready. "Cease firing" means stop shooting *immediately.* In fact, it means more than that. Cease firing means that if you are in the process of squeezing the trigger, you immediately stop, open the action, unload the rifle, and lay it down and keep your hands off it. If for some reason the rifle's action cannot be opened readily, then stop shooting, place the mechanical safety on, and lay your rifle down. Immediately let the range officer know that your gun is loaded. When you hear the "cease firing" command, absolutely do not fire the shot.

Depending upon the shooting facility, the number of people shooting, the type of shooting equipment being used, or other variables, additional commands may be used. Generally these additional commands direct the flow of shooters to and from the firing line, provide necessary instructions, or inform the shooters of time remaining.

Regardless of the shooting conditions, you have an important responsibility. If you see an unsafe situation in which someone could get hurt, then it is your responsibility to call "Cease firing." Don't wait for the range officer. Remember, anyone can call "Cease Firing." Always use common sense.

Care of Your Rifle

Your rifle is a piece of precision equipment. Like any item of value, it must be given proper care if it is to operate correctly and safely. Unlike many other items of sports equipment, your rifle is built to last a lifetime. And it will—if you care for it regularly.

Cleaning

Ideally, you should make a habit of cleaning your rifle each time it is used. A rifle that is cleaned regularly will shoot more accurately and reliably. Cleaning also preserves the finish and value of the rifle. Cleaning is essential when the rifle has been stored for an extended period or has been exposed to dirt or moisture. Don't start shooting with a dirty gun; be sure it is cleaned thoroughly before use.

As you begin to clean your rifle, first make sure the action is open, and all ammunition removed from the area. To assure absolute safety, the action should always be kept open during cleaning.

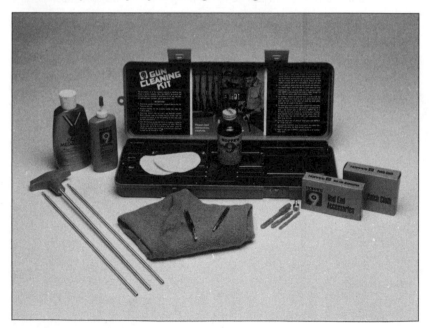

Six basic materials are needed to clean a rifle:

1. Cleaning rod with bore brush and attachment to hold patches (must be proper size for the bore of the rifle)

2. Cloth patches

3. Bore cleaning solvent

4. Light gun oil

5. Clean cloth

6. Small brush

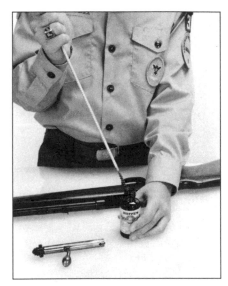

Steps in Cleaning

1. Place bore brush on cleaning rod, wet with cleaning solvent, and work it back and forth in the bore to loosen residue and fouling.

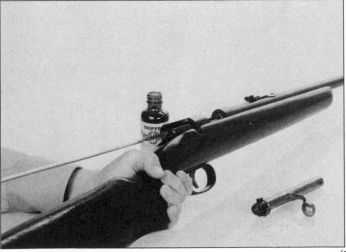

109742

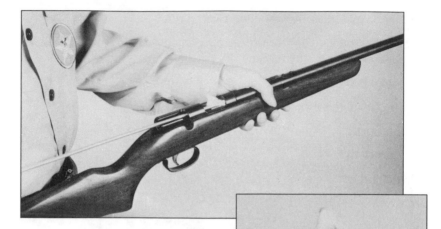

2. To remove the loosened residue and fouling, run a series of patches through it until they appear clean. Finally, push a lightly oiled patch through the bore. Repeat steps one and two if the patches don't come out clean.

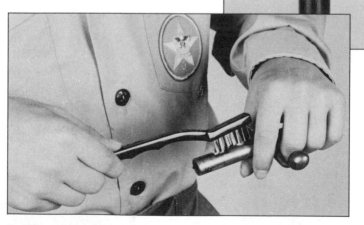

3. Clean any remaining foreign material from the rifle and the action with a small brush or cloth.

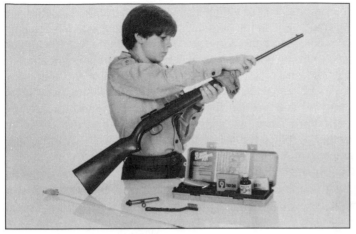

4. Wipe all exposed metal surfaces with a silicone or lightly oiled cloth.

To avoid causing rust after the rifle is cleaned, don't touch the metal. Instead, handle the gun by the stock. Don't neglect your ammunition either. Sand or dirt collected on the ammunition can damage the chamber or the bore of your rifle. Check it for foreign material before using.

When cleaning a gun that is not fired by gunpowder, such as a pellet rifle, you'll probably want to occasionally clean the bore. And, with any gun, you'll want to keep it clean and rust-free on all exposed surfaces. Follow the manufacturer's instructions.

Repairs

Beginning shooters should leave repairs to experts. If your rifle isn't functioning properly, don't use it, and don't try to fix it yourself until you are qualified to do so. Take your rifle to a professional gunsmith or have it sent back to the manufacturer for repairs.

Storing Firearms

Before you decide how and where you are going to keep your gun and ammunition, consider safety, storage conditions, access by others, and your personal needs. Many people are naturally intrigued by guns, and the temptation to pick one up is very real for adults and children alike. That could spell trouble if the person is too young or inexperienced to handle the gun safely. Security is another factor. Unfortunately, guns are often desirable booty for thieves.

For all these reasons, it's wise to find a secure and convenient location for your shooting equipment. Many manufacturers offer fine wooden cabinets to display and secure your guns. Some gun owners prefer to have their guns in locked metal vaults or storage places where they are out of sight and out of reach. If you choose storage that requires a lock, be sure you keep your keys in a place where casual visitors and youngsters aren't likely to find them.

Always store your guns so that they are not accessible to untrained or unauthorized persons. When removing a firearm for handling or cleaning, always remember to follow the safety rules, and double check to be sure the gun is empty.

Ammunition should be kept in a cool, dry place. Many rifle owners prefer to store their guns and ammunition separately to minimize the chance of an accident.

Many aspects of safety are not covered here. Think about a few examples and what you would do about them. For example, when hunting in the field, you come to a fence. How can you and your gun get safely to the other side? Remember to open the action and remove all ammunition. Place your gun carefully on the ground under the lower wire of the fence. Then walk to a fence post away from your gun. Climb the post and cross to the other side. Then, carefully pick up your gun in such a way that the muzzle is never aimed at you. Now you can put the ammunition back in the gun and continue hunting.

Rifle Shooting Fundamentals

Now that you know how your rifle works, how to handle it safely, and how to care for it, you're ready to learn how to shoot it. As you'll soon see, there's much more to it than just pulling the trigger.

Learning to shoot a rifle accurately is much the same as being introduced to any other skill. In soccer, for instance, the beginner is taught the basic skills—like kicking, passing, and shooting—before taking to the field and beginning actual play. Likewise, it is the same with rifle shooting. To shoot a rifle accurately, you must first learn and master the basic skills of *shooting position, shot preparation, sight picture control, trigger control,* and *follow through.* These skills are known as the fundamentals of rifle shooting because they must be performed every time you shoot a rifle.

Once you've learned the fundamental shooting skills, you'll be ready to learn how to apply them to various rifle shooting activities for a lifetime of fun and challenges.

There are five rifle shooting fundamentals:

1. Shooting position
2. Shot preparation
3. Sight picture control
4. Trigger control
5. Follow through

Before you can sight your rifle or begin shooting, a major decision must be made. Are you right-eye or left-eye dominant? You can be right-handed or left-handed, but that doesn't determine your strongest eye. To find your dominant eye, extend your hands in front of you. Put your hands together. Form a small opening between them. Keep both eyes open, and look through the opening at an object in the distance.

Then move your hands backward until they touch your face—all the while keeping the object in sight. Now close one eye. Do you still see the object? If so, the open eye is your dominant one. If you don't see the object, open your closed eye and close the other. You will see the object. You must shoulder your rifle on the same side as your dominant eye.

Shooting Position

The shooting position is simply the posture of your body and rifle during the act of shooting. There are several positions and position variations that are used in rifle shooting. A knowledgeable rifle shooter should know five basic rifle shooting positions—prone, kneeling, standing, bench rest, and sitting.

Prone position.

Kneeling position.

Standing position.

Bench rest position.

Sitting position.

Even though the position of the body can vary greatly, the position of the rifle basically remains the same.

One might ask, "Why so many positions?" Surely one or two of those positions are better than the others. The truth is each position is best suited for certain conditions. The position you choose depends on the kind of shooting, the terrain, shooting time, and target difficulty. In addition, the traditions and rules of the sport have greatly influenced the established positions and when they are used.

The importance of building rifle shooting skill on a foundation of good positions cannot be overemphasized. The position must give you a solid, steady hold on the target. A good shooting position involves the position of the body and the position of the rifle.

Position of the Body

The position of the body is the arrangement of the head, torso, arms, and legs, and their relationship to the target. Positioning the body is the first step in assuming every shooting position. Three conditions are essential for a good position. First, you must be *comfortable* and *relaxed.* This means attaining as natural a body position as possible without straining your muscles. Second, the position must provide *maximum bone support*—to the greatest extent possible, use bones and not muscles to support the body and rifle. If you rely primarily on muscles to support the weight of the rifle, you will have a hard time relaxing and keeping the rifle steady. Third, *your position* must be *aligned with the target.* If the preceding conditions are met, the rifle will settle into a *natural point of aim.* (The whole position must then be adjusted to align that natural point of aim on the target.) Never muscle the rifle on target.

Position of the Rifle

The position of the rifle involves the proper positioning of the rifle to the body. The rifle must be positioned against the shoulder so that you can look through the sights with your dominant eye, comfortably and naturally. Alignment with the eye of the sights is essential to proper rifle position.

Correct hand and index finger placement on the rifle grip and trigger is necessary to correctly hold the rifle and pull the trigger. Grasp the grip of the stock firmly with the lower three fingers, lightly resting the thumb on the top of the stock. Place the hand so that the index finger can pull the trigger straight to the rear.

The fore-end should rest in the left hand. It is best not to grip or squeeze the fore-end. However, with more powerful calibers it may be necessary to grip the fore-end to maintain control when firing.

All position descriptions and photos in this pamphlet are for right-handed shooters unless designated otherwise. Shooters that shoot from the left shoulder (left-handed) will need to reverse the position information.

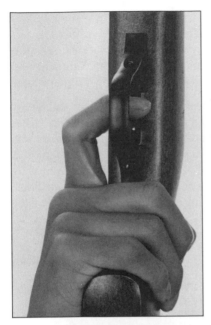

◄The finger placement should allow the trigger to be pulled straight to the rear.

The trigger finger should be clear of the stock so it will not press on the stock while pulling the trigger.
▼

Shot Preparation

Once in position, there are two actions necessary to prepare to fire a shot: aiming and breath control.

Aiming

Aiming, simply stated, is the process of lining up the rifle with the target. It involves the alignment of your eye, the rear sight, the front sight (or scope), and the target. Aiming is done in two steps—the first is sight alignment; the second is sight picture. The most critical step in rifle shooting is sight picture.

- Sight alignment is the relationship between the eye, the rear sight, and the front sight or scope. Consistent and proper sight alignment is necessary for accurate aiming. When using open sights with a post or bead front sight, you have correct sight alignment when the front sight is centered in the rear sight notch and the top edge of the front sight is even with the top of the rear sight. With aperture or peep sights, correct sight alignment is achieved when the front sight ring or the top edge of the front sight

AIMING OPEN SIGHTS

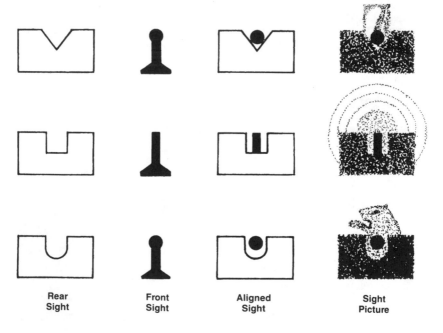

| Rear
Sight | Front
Sight | Aligned
Sight | Sight
Picture |

AIMING APERTURE SIGHTS

post is centered in the rear sight aperture. When using a telescopic sight, you achieve proper sight alignment by positioning your eye so that you can clearly see the entire field of view when looking through the scope.

• Sight picture is the relationship between the aligned sights or scope and the target. Sight picture will vary according to the type of sights you are using and the kind of target you are shooting. An aligned bead front sight should be aimed at the center of the target. The top edge of the post front sight is centered on the target bull's-eye. The target for aperture sights should be centered inside an aligned front-sight ring. When the correct sight picture is obtained, the front sight should be clearly defined while the target and rear sight remain slightly out of focus, as shown in the illustrations. A scope reticle (cross hairs) is simply centered on the target.

Breath Control

Breath control means stopping your breathing before you fire a shot. Breathing causes your body to move. That's fine, unless you happen to be ready to fire a shot. Continuing to breathe makes it impossible to maintain a steady sight picture. Before firing the shot, be sure you are relaxed and comfortable. Then simply exhale normally and stop breathing. This will assist you in aiming by reducing the movement of your body and rifle in relation to the target. Generally you should hold your breath no longer than 6–8 seconds. If you are not able to fire the shot within this time, take a breath or two, relax, and start the process again.

Sight Picture Control

Sight picture control means keeping the aligned sights or scope reticle aimed as closely as possible on the center of the target. It is the most important period in the firing of a shot. Even though you assume a proper and relaxed position and stop breathing, you will still notice movement in the sight picture. This movement is natural. Only from a support, such as on a bench rest, can a shooter come close to eliminating it completely. You can, however, control and reduce the amount of movement by concentrating on achieving the proper sight picture and holding as still as possible. You must learn to concentrate totally and consistently on sight picture control when firing.

Controlling the movement in your sight picture is not something you can learn in one or two shooting sessions. All other fundamentals of shooting can be learned in a fairly short time, but sight picture control is practiced by champion shooters for years without achieving perfection. Absolute perfection may not be possible. However, beginning shooters will notice rapid improvement in their sight picture if they concentrate on achieving good sight picture control and practice regularly.

Trigger Control

Once you have your best sight picture, gently pull the trigger straight back in a smooth, controlled motion until the rifle fires. This process is referred to as trigger control. The key is to pull the trigger so smoothly that it does not disturb your sight picture. Initially, you may not be able to cause the rifle to fire when the sight picture is best. But with practice, as you become familiar with your rifle's trigger, you will be able to fire the rifle when the sight picture is right.

Remember that during this firing process you must continue to concentrate on sight picture control.

Follow-through

Follow-through is the act of continuing to maintain breath control, sight picture control, and trigger control immediately following the shot. Allow enough time for the rifle to return to its normal position after the recoil. This will minimize the possibility that any sudden movement (during the split second between the time the shot is fired and the bullet leaves the muzzle) will disturb the sight picture and radically change the bullet's path.

Zeroing a Rifle

Sights are on a rifle for two purposes. You should be careful not to confuse the two. The primary purpose is to enable you to point the rifle at exactly the same spot on the target each time. This will result in your shot holes being very closely grouped together on the target—a "tight group." The first and most difficult thing for you to learn is how to shoot a tight group. You must learn how to do precise work with this precision instrument.

The second purpose of rifle sights is far less important and is learned fairly easily. This second purpose is to put the center of your tight group on the center of the target, which will give you the highest score and the best chance of hitting right in the center. We will be talking mostly about peep sights, as they are practically always used in target shooting.

Your sights can be moved sideways and up and down to allow for changes in wind, distance, light, and other factors.

The first purpose of the sights—ensuring exact, precise alignment—is called "sighting" or sight alignment. The second purpose of the sights—the mechanical movement of the sights to center the group in the center of the target—is called "zeroing." Sights on your peep sight are usually set by turning knobs, and there are gradations on the sight so that they can be carefully adjusted and the setting can be recorded.

If you want to hit the target consistently in the center of the target, you must shoot a small group and adjust the group to the center of the target. Since shooting a small group is the difficult job, and sighting is a big part of it, let's talk first about sight setting, sight alignment, and sight picture.

There are three parts to the sighting system: a rear sight, the front sight, and the target. On the peep sight, the rear aperture is a small hole in a metal disk. The size of the disk isn't important, and the size of the hole in the disk isn't important as long as it is big enough. Take a good look at your peep sight—this is probably the last time you will look at it. In the future you will look through the hole, and not at it.

The front sight is a short metal post with a flat top and straight sides. You look through the rear peep at the front sight. Center the top of the front sight in the rear peep, concentrating on looking at the post. This is proper sight alignment. Practice this until it becomes second nature.

The third part of the sighting system is the target. With the front sight centered in the peep, try to get the round bull's-eye of the target sitting gently on top of the post. If all goes well, the bull will sit quietly on top of the front sight, waiting for you to shoot it. However, you'll quickly notice the bull will appear to be bouncing and dancing around, never holding still for a moment. Don't worry about this. It happens to all of us. Also, you aren't sure the sights are set in such a way that they'll get the bullet directly to the target. Only by shooting can you learn this. In this sight adjusting shooting, you want to be sure your rifle is as steady as possible, so use the bench rest position.

The Bench Rest Position

This position is the steadiest and will give the best indication of the groups you will fire. You should start shooting in this position from a table. You'll need a sandbag or other solid support to place under the fore-end of the rifle. The support helps hold your rifle steady and enables you to concentrate on learning how to shoot a good shot. If a table or bench isn't available, place the sandbag or support on the ground and use a supported prone position.

There are four basic steps to follow when learning any shooting position. Use them to learn the bench rest position.

Step 1 Study the position. Learn what a good bench rest position looks like by studying the pictures in this book.

Step 2 Practice the position without the rifle. Learn to put your feet, legs, body, and arms in the correct position by getting into position behind the table. Practice this until you are comfortable with the position.

Step 3 Practice the position with the rifle. Add the rifle to the position you have already assumed. Again concentrate on becoming comfortable and familiar with the position.

Step 4 Align the position with the target. Adjust the position so that the rifle points naturally at the target.

Position of the body ►

▼ Position of the rifle

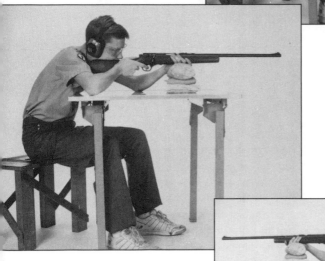

Left-handed position ►

Getting into Position

1. Take a seat facing the table.

2. Grasp rifle with right hand and position elbows on table.

3. Lay rifle across left hand and rest left hand on sandbag.

4. Position rifle against face and shoulder so that the dominant eye can look through the sights comfortably and naturally.

Align Position with Target

1. Make vertical adjustments by adjusting the height of the sandbag support.

2. Make horizontal adjustments by moving the sandbag support left or right on the table.

Note: Reverse right and left directions if left eye is dominant.

The Trigger

When firing a rifle, the trigger must be pulled to release the firing mechanism without moving the gun. In larger calibers, the gun makes considerable noise and may kick your shoulder a bit. The common reaction is to tighten up just before the trigger is pulled to resist the kick and the noise. This leads to jerking the trigger, resulting in wide shots and unaccountable misses.

Your rifle will normally be used against stationary targets. There's no rush about pulling the trigger. With this precision instrument you try to put all your shots in the same hole. The slightest thing that interferes with this precision will reduce your score. The rifle trigger must be pulled with a rather slow, gradual increase in pressure by your trigger finger. You will find that the sights wobble around, and only occasionally will your sights be lined up the way you think they should. The great temptation is to yank the trigger just when things look good. This may give you a center shot, but more likely it will give you many wide ones. Don't yank the trigger. Even if you don't yank the shot, you may find that you have a tendency to hold the rifle with a grip of iron, in an attempt to hold it still and reduce the wobble. This won't work either. Breath control will help control this wobble.

Dry Firing

The best way to learn the shooting fundamentals is with a dry run. A technique called dry firing is used to practice before actually using live ammunition. Dry firing consists of closing the rifle's action on an empty (unloaded) chamber, then practicing the steps involved in firing the shot just as if the rifle were actually loaded. To do this, get into position with your rifle on the target, making sure you are comfortable and relaxed. When you feel ready, begin aiming and control your breathing. Concentrate on controlling (reducing) the movement of the sight picture. When it looks good, squeeze the trigger smoothly to the rear.

Dry fire several shots to get the feel of how much pressure is required to smoothly move the trigger without disturbing the sight picture. This requires total concentration on the sight picture at the moment of firing.

If you are using a muzzle-loader, you will have to take protective steps to prevent damage to the nipple or the flint. With the percussion rifle, you can prevent nipple damage by placing one or two rubber or neoprene faucet washers over the nipple. On a flintlock, you can prevent wear and tear by simply removing the flint and replacing it with a comparable-sized piece of cut hardwood. This will allow you to experience the fall of the hammer and the action of the frizzen without regard to safety problems or wear and tear on your flint or frizzen.

Live Firing

It's now time to try the real thing with live ammunition. Shoot three to five shots at the target. Be sure to apply the same fundamentals as you applied during dry firing. If you've been consistent in applying the fundamentals correctly, your shots should form a cluster or shot group on the target. At this point, don't worry about where the group is on the target. Your only concern now should be whether the shots fall together in a group. Shoot several groups. With practice your groups should become smaller and smaller. If your shots are scattered all over the target, do more dry firing and review the fundamentals. Also, be sure your sights are tight on the gun. Any movement there can cause wild shots.

Sight Adjustment

Once you are shooting good groups with shots placed closely together, you are ready to adjust your sights to move your shot groups to the center of the target. This adjustment is made by moving the peep, reticle, or rear sight in the same direction you want your shot to move. For example, if your group is high and to the left, move the rear sight down and to the right. Most adjustment knobs are marked to show which way the knob should be turned to move a shot group in a particular direction. The instructions with most sights will tell how far one "click" or gradation of sight adjustment should move a shot at a specific distance.

Test your calculations by firing another group. The goal is to have the center of your group in the center of the target. If you're still off, continue making adjustments until the group is in the center of the target. Also remember that your sights will likely need to be adjusted if you shoot at a target at a different distance.

Shots on a target can be read according to the face of a clock. The shot group above is at 2 o'clock in the 8 ring.

Shooting Positions

A number of positions may be used in rifle shooting. We've already described the bench rest position that you use to zero your rifle. It's now time to move to other basic positions: standing, prone, kneeling, and sitting. While you will be doing all of your actual shooting for the merit badge from the bench rest position, the requirements also ask you to demonstrate these other positions.

As we have seen, rifle shooting is a precision sport. The foundation is a solid, steady position. The general rule in rifle shooting is to use as few muscles as possible, and to use them as little as possible. Instead of using your muscles, which get tired and shaky, use your bones as much as you can to support the rifle. Remember, three conditions are essential for a good position. First, you must be comfortable and relaxed. Second, the position must provide maximum bone support—to the extent possible, use bones and not muscles to support the body and rifle. Third, your position must be aligned with the target. If these conditions are met, the rifle will settle into a natural point of aim.

The Standing Position

This is probably the most natural and most often used position. It is the quickest and easiest position to assume. Since it provides the highest and least stable support for the rifle, it is also the most challenging position to learn. There are two variations of the standing position. These are the free arm and the arm rest position. The type of shooting you are doing determines the variation you will use.

Free Arm Standing Position

This position is used when the time available to fire a shot is very short or when the target is moving, as in hunting. Shooters who use this position should be sure they have sufficient arm strength or a rifle that is light enough to hold up comfortably. You will find that when shooting from this position there will be a great deal of wobble in the sight picture. Unlike the bench rest position, there is little firm support at the fore-end of the stock, which allows the muzzle to move quite easily. Continued practice in holding your gun in this position is the best way to overcome this wobble.

Position Characteristics:

Position of the Body

1. Feet are shoulder width apart.

2. Body weight is distributed equally on both feet.

3. Head and body are erect.

4. Left arm is free from the body.

Position of the Rifle

5. Left hand under fore-end supports weight of rifle.

6. Right hand grasps rifle grip.

7. Butt of stock is positioned against shoulder so rifle sight is at eye level.

Getting into Position

◄ 1. Hold rifle in both hands; move to firing point.

Stand sideways to target. ►

3. Grasp fore-end between thumb and forefinger of left hand with wrist straight.

4. Raise rifle to eye level and position it against shoulder.

Align with Target

1. Make vertical adjustments by varying the position of the left arm.

2. Make horizontal adjustments by moving the feet.

Arm Rest Standing Position

The arm rest standing position is used when a higher degree of stability and accuracy is required, as in most target events. This position is normally steadier and provides more support than the free arm variation. Shooters using a rifle that is too heavy to comfortably hold up in the free arm position should use the arm rest standing position.

Position Characteristics:

Position of the Body

1. Feet are shoulder width apart.

2. Body weight is distributed equally on both feet.

3. Body bends back away from rifle.

4. Head is erect.

5. Left arm rests on side or hip.

Position of the Rifle

6. Left hand supports the rifle; wrist is straight.

7. Right hand grasps the rifle grip.

8. Butt of stock is positioned against shoulder so rifle sights are at eye level.

Getting into Position

1. Hold rifle in both hands; move to firing point.

2. Stand sideways to target.

3. Grasp fore-end between thumb and forefinger of left hand with wrist straight.

4. Raise rifle to eye level and position against shoulder, resting left arm against body.

Align Position with Target

1. Make vertical adjustments by varying the position of the left arm against the body.

2. Make horizontal adjustments by moving the feet.

The Prone Position

Next to the bench rest position, this is the steadiest of the positions shown in this manual. Both elbows and the entire body are in contact with the ground, thus providing a wide area of support.

Position Characteristics:

Position of the Body

1. Body lies facing the target and angled slightly to the left.

2. Left elbow is extended forward of the body.

3. Right knee is bent slightly.

Position of Rifle

4. Rifle fore-end rests on left hand.

5. Right hand grasps rifle grip.

6. Butt of stock is positioned against shoulder so rifle sight is at eye level.

Getting into Position

1. Hold rifle in both hands; move to firing point.
2. With rifle in left hand, get down on knees.

3. Lower body to floor (prone position).

4. Extend the left elbow forward.

Left-handed position

5. Raise rifle to eye level and position against the shoulder.

Align Position with Target

1. Make vertical adjustments by moving the left hand forward (lowers the rifle) or to the rear (raises the rifle) on the fore-end.

2. Make horizontal adjustments by rotating position left or right around the left elbow.

Kneeling Position

In addition to being an important target position, the kneeling position is particularly useful in the field. It's quick to assume, steadier than standing, and provides the clearance necessary to shoot over terrain such as tall weeds or brush.

Position Characteristics:

Position of the Body

1. Body sits on heel of right foot.

2. Lower left leg vertical.

3. Left elbow rests on left knee.

Position of Rifle ▲

4. Rifle fore-end rests in left hand.

5. Right hand grasps rifle grip.

6. Butt of stock is positioned against shoulder so rifle sight is at eye level.

◀**Getting into Position**

1. Hold rifle in both hands; move to firing point.

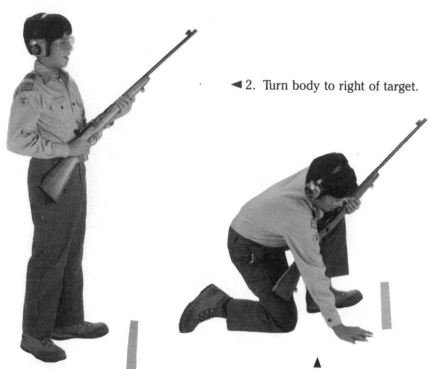

◄ 2. Turn body to right of target.

▲

3. Drop onto right knee and sit on right foot.

◄ 4. Adjust left leg so that lower leg is vertical.

5. Place left elbow on left knee.

6. Raise rifle to eye level and
   position against shoulder.

Left-handed positions

Align Position with Target

1. Make vertical adjustments by moving left hand forward (lowers rifle) or to the rear (raises rifle) on the fore-end.

2. Make horizontal adjustments by rotating the position left or right around the left foot.

   In kneeling, most of your body weight should be on the right foot. You can place a tightly rolled strip of carpet, jacket, cylindrical cushion, or similar support (kneeling roll) under the right foot for additional support and comfort.

The Sitting Position

This is a stable position because it provides support for both elbows, which helps to steady the rifle. For hunters, sitting, like kneeling, provides more ground clearance than the prone position.

Position Characteristics:

Position of the Body

1. Body sits on the ground.

2. Legs are extended from the body with ankles crossed.

3. Elbows rest on legs just in front of knees.

Position of the Rifle

4. Rifle fore-end rests on left hand.

5. Right hand grasps rifle grip.

6. Butt of stock is positioned against shoulder so rifle sight is at eye level.

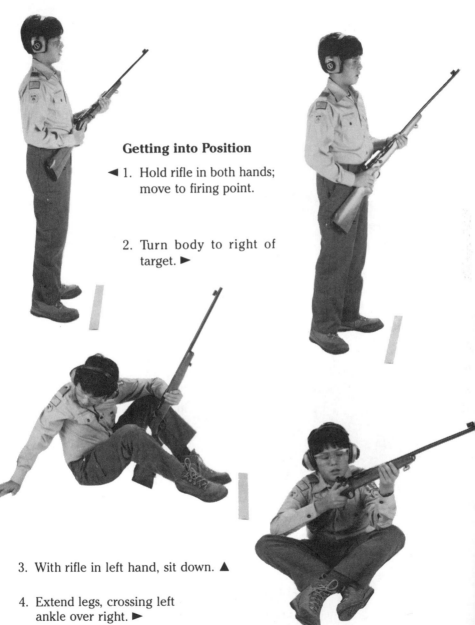

Getting into Position

◀ 1. Hold rifle in both hands; move to firing point.

2. Turn body to right of target. ▶

3. With rifle in left hand, sit down. ▲

4. Extend legs, crossing left ankle over right. ▶

◄ 5. Place elbows forward of knees.

◄ 6. Raise rifle to eye level and position against shoulder.

Align Position with Target

1. Make vertical adjustments by moving the left hand forward (lowers rifle) or to the rear (raises rifle) on the fore-end.

2. Make horizontal adjustments by rotating the position left or right around buttocks.

A variation of the sitting position

Left-handed position

Scoring

When you've answered the questions and done the demonstrations called for in the requirements, you're ready for the shooting. The gun, the targets, and the distances vary in the options offered for the cartridge rifle, the air rifle, and the muzzle-loader.

The shooting position is the bench rest or supported position. The objective in shooting is to get your cluster of shots all within the center. This should not be too difficult, once you have zeroed in on your sights.

Look at the minimum required scores as indicated for the A-17 or TQ-1 targets for the .22 rifle. The requirement says that you must shoot five groups with five shots in each group, and that the minimum score for any of the shots is eight. If one of the other targets is used, the minimum changes. For the A-32 target, the minimum value awarded for each shot is nine; for the A-36 target, the minimum is six. This may seem complicated, but once you examine a target you'll see how your shots are scored.

Once your shot group is zeroed in on the target, and you're shooting from the bench rest position, each minimum score fired must be in the range listed to meet the requirements. It sounds somewhat complicated, but it really isn't.

Choosing a Rifle

Buying a rifle of your own can be something you'll remember all of your life. But picking the right one can be tough. Your rifle selection process should include a review of laws in your area that pertain to the purchase, ownership, use, possession, and carrying of firearms. These laws vary widely according to community and state. The following guidelines will help:

Action

Any action is good that can be kept open during handling and that permits easy visual access to the chamber and to the magazine, if it has one.

Trigger

The release pressure must be greater than 3 pounds on a single-stage trigger. The final release pressure must also be greater than 3 pounds on a two-stage trigger. A two-stage trigger has a take-up, or movement, stage before the final stage and a heavier final stage where the trigger should not move perceptibly. The "greater than 3 pounds" release pressure must be in the final stage.

Weight

This will probably be from 4½ to 6 pounds.

Barrel

Standard for a Scout-age shooter is 18 to 22 inches in length.

Stock

This is best if adjustable in length. About 12 to 13½ inches from trigger to butt is about right. The stock or grip should fit your hand and be located to allow proper placement of the finger on the trigger. A universal stock for either right- or left-handers is preferred.

Sights

Any type of rear sight that can be easily adjusted both horizontally and vertically is fine. If you are planning to use a scope, one of six power or less with internal adjustments is ideal.

You might be able to use a rifle range in your town or at Scout camp. At these, you'll probably be using a rifle provided at the range. This is fine. Just be sure to sight your borrowed rifle to your own satisfaction.

When buying a rifle, you'll have a wide selection. But you'll probably choose a rifle of the same size and caliber as the one you used to earn your merit badge.

Your local library or bookstore is a good place to begin your study. A visit to a local sporting goods or gun specialty store is also a must. Find a truly interested salesperson who will explain the features of the models you're studying. Be specific about your interests, plans for use, and budget. In all you do, take your time. Don't buy on impulse or because of a quick sales pitch.

Select a Rifle That Fits

The main part of a rifle's fit is in the stock. Most manufacturers sell rifles with standard stock dimensions designed to fit the average-size adult. Many also produce youth models with smaller or adjustable dimensions suitable to a smaller physique.

There are two important fit considerations—the length and comb of the stock. For young people or adults with short arms or stature, standard length stocks are often too long. Measure the stock by placing the butt in the crook of your arm. If your hand reaches the pistol grip and trigger comfortably, the stock should be reasonably close to the right length. If the distance is too great, a competent gunsmith can measure the distance to be removed and refit the gun to the right size. If the distance is too short, the gunsmith can add a slip-on pad or spacer plates to lengthen it.

The comb of the stock can also be important. A comb that's too high will prevent you from properly aligning your eye with the sights. This can be fixed by either raising the height of the sights or removing wood from the comb. A comb that's too low doesn't provide support for your face when your eye is aligned with the sights. This can be corrected by using lower sights or by taping a layer of hard rubber over the comb. However, when buying a new gun, none of these alternatives should be used. Buy a rifle that fits you.

The adult rifle in the upper photo is much too big for a youngster to successfully shoot from any position. The smaller rifle is more suited for the youngster's needs.

Before You Buy

In buying a gun, answer these questions before you make your choice. If it's a used gun, take additional care in your decision.

- How do you plan to use this rifle? Is the use multipurpose or specific? What are the best caliber, weight, and sights for this use?

- Is ammunition readily available? How much will ammunition cost for the amount of shooting you plan to do?

- How much do you have, or can you spend, for the rifle?

- Have you done your homework? Have you studied manufacturers' catalogs? Have you looked at and handled the different makes available? Have you checked the accessory and special feature options?

- Is the rifle simple to operate and clean?

- Does the rifle fit you?

- Have you read the warranty or guarantee?

- Is the rifle produced by a known manufacturer? Buying quality brands will generally ensure the availability of future repairs and a good return on your investment.

- Does the rifle have a good track record for dependability?

- Are you purchasing from a reputable dealer?

- Can the sights be easily adjusted?

- Can accessories be easily added to accommodate changing shooting interests?

- What is the marketability if you decide to sell your rifle? Could you get back most of your money in a sale?

- Have you taken your time in making your choice?

Remember, the chances are good you'll keep your rifle for life.

Buying a Used Rifle

Some additional points when buying a used rifle:

- Locate the previous owner, if possible, and find out why the rifle was traded or sold.

- A poor outward appearance on a rifle generally indicates abuse or excessive wear.

- Make certain a reblue or refinish job hasn't disguised the actual past use of the rifle.

- Check the bore for bulges or excessive wear.

- Check the screw slots to determine if they have been abused during disassembly by an inexperienced person.

- Check the trigger for consistent, safe pull and smooth function.

- Check the safety to determine if it functions properly.

- Note that rifles in an original, unaltered condition tend to be of more value.

- Secure advice from an expert on guns regarding this rifle's market value.

- Check the wood in the stock for type, quality, and hairline cracks.

- Shoot the rifle, if possible, before buying.

- Be certain the rifle is legally owned by the seller.

- You usually get what you pay for! Beware of deals that are too good to be true—they usually are.

Sight-in Your Rifle

Rifles that come directly from the manufacturer or have been used by other people must be sighted-in for your eye. This is also known as "zeroing" the rifle. Zero is the sight adjustment that will allow the bullet to strike the target at the desired point of aim.

Follow the steps outlined on sighting in the chapter titled "Zeroing a Rifle."

Remember, too, that different ammunition, shooting distances, and shooting positions can change the zero and therefore require additional sight adjustments.

Air Rifles

Air rifles provide a beginning shooter with a gun (they are not toys) that is inexpensive to buy. In addition, the ammunition is much cheaper than the cartridge type.

Instructions for safety for all guns apply to air guns. The shooting positions apply, as do instructions in sighting the rifle. You probably won't have a peep sight with your air guns, but continued practice will tell you exactly where to sight-in for the bull's-eye.

BB Gun

This is the simplest and least expensive of all rifles. It operates by a lever or pump that compresses a spring that has a plunger head attached to it. When the trigger is pulled, the spring releases and sends a blast of air up the bore behind the BB shot. The bore on a BB gun isn't rifled, so accuracy drops off as distance to the target increases. The controlled average muzzle velocity of the BB is around 300 feet per second. This gives good accuracy at short distances. The Boy Scouts of America has accepted and approved the BB gun for the Rifle Shooting merit badge.

Pellet Gun

These guns also operate by air. Rifle-barreled CO_2 gas, pneumatic (pump-up), and spring-operated air guns fire skirted lead pellets at varying velocities, usually between the ranges of 300 to 600 feet per second. The most common caliber of the pellets is .22 or .177. Because they have lower velocities than the .22-caliber gun, these gas and air guns are used at an approved range distance of 25 feet on the TQ-5 target or 33 feet or 10 meters on the AR-1 target. These targets, including the TQ-5 for BB guns, have been developed by the NRA to have bull's-eyes ratioed in size so that the difficulty of meeting the shooting requirements will be comparable to the .22-caliber firearm 50-foot-range approved targets.

The advantages, in addition to cost, are the lack of explosive noise on firing, no recoil, and less distance needed between firing line and target, which make these guns great for use in a large room or outdoors.

The air gun is a great way to practice at a reasonable cost, and certainly can qualify you for the shooting section of the badge. Care and cleaning of your gun are covered in the chapter titled "Care of Your Rifle."

Olympic Games and Shooting

Olympic-style shooting evolved from the European tradition of shooting. It is characterized by uniform courses of fire and strict regulations governing clothing, equipment, and firearms to ensure the uniformity of these items used in international competition.

Shooting is governed worldwide by the International Shooting Union (UIT), with headquarters in Munich, West Germany. The National Rifle Association of America is recognized by the U.S. Olympic Committee as the national governing body for the shooting sports in this country.

The following rifle sports are fired in the Olympics:

Men's Free Rifle Prone ('English Match')

This event is shot at 50 meters with .22 caliber rifles weighing no more than 17.6 pounds (8 kilograms), including accessories. The match is fired strictly from the prone (lying down) position. Shooters fire one shot per target, and as with all rifle events described here, metallic sights are used.

Course of fire: 60 shots in 1 hour and 45 minutes

Perfect score: 600

Target: Bull's-eye target with a center 10 ring approximately the size of a dime (.48 inches)

Men's Free Rifle 3-Position

Shot with a .22 caliber rifle weighing no more than 17.6 pounds (8 kilograms) including accessories, this event is fired in three positions: prone, standing, and kneeling. One shot per target is fired from the 50-meter line.

Course of fire: 120 shots—40 shots per position, with the following time allowances: 1 hour and 15 minutes for prone, 1 hour and 45 minutes for standing, and 1 hour and 30 minutes for kneeling

Perfect score: 1200

Target: Bull's-eye with a center 10 ring approximately the size of a dime

Women's Standard Rifle 3-Position

Open to women only, this match is almost identical to the men's event described above. Competitors face certain restrictions on their firearms. Standard rifles with a maximum weight of 11 pounds must be used. The use of the following accessories is not permitted: butt hooks, palm rests, thumbhole stocks, and spirit levels. The event is fired from the 50-meter line in the kneeling, standing, and prone positions.

Course of fire: 20 shots per position, totaling 60 shots. Time limit is 2 hours and 30 minutes; individual positions are not timed.

Perfect score: 600

Target: Bull's-eye with a center 10 ring approximately the size of a dime

Men's Air Rifle

For this event, match rules permit the use of any air- or gas-powered rifle having a bore of 4.5 millimeters (.177 caliber), and weighing not more than 5 kilograms (11 pounds). The match is fired from a distance of 10 meters, in the standing position. Shooters fire one shot per target.

Course of fire: 60 shots in 2 hours and 15 minutes

Perfect score: 600

Target: Bull's-eye target with a center 10 ring measuring 1 millimeter

Women's Air Rifle

This event is fired with the same type of rifle used in the men's event. The match differs from men's air rifle only in the number of shots fired and the time limit for firing. Shooters fire one shot per target.

Course of fire: 40 shots in 1 hour and 30 minutes

Perfect score: 400

Target: Bull's-eye target whose center is the size of the head of a pin

For additional information, write to:

NRA Shooting Sports
U.S. Olympic Training Center
1750 East Boulder Street
Colorado Springs, CO 80909

Conservation and Hunting

Wildlife biologists have long recognized that there are two major factors in game management.

The first is that you can't stockpile wildlife. With few exceptions, a given piece of ground can support only a given number of one type of wildlife. If you decide you would like to have more game of a certain kind in that area and you stock it with additional wildlife, what will happen? If you go back in a year or so, you won't find any increase in the number of animals. Starvation, disease, or predators will have taken the extra ones.

The second factor of importance is that nature overproduces every year— produces far more animals than the area can support. And, as we saw above, the excess is lost—nature's way of making sure that there are enough animals each year for breeding and for ensuring that only the strongest strains survive for reproduction. For example, only 8 percent of young rabbits grow to breeding age.

These principles apply despite what you do to the animals. If you put extra animals in the area, more animals than normal will die. If you kill a few extra animals, the remaining stock will soon bring the population up to the normal figure. Wildlife management experts try to arrange the hunting seasons and the bag limits so that any surplus can be harvested by hunters. Hunting regulations they set ensure that hunters don't take too many animals. Far better that the hunter should get the healthful outdoor recreation—and the meat—harvesting the surplus than to lose it to disease, starvation, and other natural causes.

Occasionally an animal population will grow too large. For a few years there will be a larger carryover than the land can support properly. When it is obvious that the carryover is too large, it is most important to increase the harvest and get the herd down to a safe size for the land. Game managers will often increase the length of the hunting season and increase the bag limit to accomplish this. Hunters harvest game that would otherwise be lost to natural causes. They help nature bring an overlarge herd down to safe size.

The real problem for game animals is what man has done, and is doing, to the habitat in which these animals live. Replacing woods, fields, and marshes with subdivisions, shopping centers, superhighways, industrial complexes, or airports leads to reduced numbers of game animals.

Hunting Regulations

Each state has its own hunting regulations. They are usually issued by the state fish and game department, conservation department, or a similar organization that controls hunting and fishing. You can obtain copies of the regulations by writing to the correct department at your state capital. Locally, you can usually get these from a sporting goods store or hardware store where hunting licenses are sold. Your merit badge counselor can help you with this, too.

There are many differences in the state game laws. Hunting in Kansas is unlike hunting in California or New York. Differences in geography, population, and game types call for different game laws. Even within a certain state there will be differences in some game laws. Certain areas or counties may have different regulations because of local conditions.

In hunting language, "big game" usually refers to deer, bear, antelope, elk, and moose. Small game usually includes rabbits, raccoons, opossums, squirrels, and the like.

Many states have regulations regarding the use or carrying of guns when hunting. These are designed to protect you and others in the hunting neighborhood. Such laws might prohibit carrying a loaded gun in a car, or shooting from a car, or shooting near buildings. Many states control the type of gun that can be used for some kinds of hunting.

Most states require hunters to carry a hunting license. This controls the game harvest, and the fees provide funds for development and game management. To get a hunting license for the first time, many states require the hunter to satisfactorily complete the hunter safety course initially developed by the National Rifle Association and now controlled by each state's hunter education program. These courses are given by volunteer instructors. Even if your state doesn't require you to take such a course, it is certainly worth your time to take it before you start hunting. You'll find it interesting, and if you've earned your Rifle Shooting merit badge, you won't find it too difficult.

Sportsmanship

Sportsmanship is basic to hunting safety and to conservation. The true sportsman follows the Golden Rule. You treat others the way you would like to have them treat you.

The sportsman knows and always follows the rules for safe gun handling at home, on the range, and in the field. He knows and strictly follows the laws regarding possession and use of firearms. The sportsman knows and strictly follows the rules and regulations of competitive shooting. He knows and follows the letter and spirit of the hunting regulations.

The sportsman is considerate of the landowner whose property he may be using. He asks permission to hunt on the property. He leaves gates as he finds them. He is careful not to damage fences or other property. He doesn't litter the area with trash.

The accomplishment of taking game during the hunt is only part of the experience. Enjoying the outdoors, seeing wildlife, and stalking game are also pleasurable parts of the hunt.

The sportsman is careful of his target, not only for safety but to avoid senseless destruction. He doesn't shoot powerline insulators, pipeline valves, signs, or similar property. He confines his shots to proper targets.

The sportsman is careful of the area beyond his target to ensure that bullets that miss the target or ricochet don't travel on to cause damage.

The sportsman, when hunting in the field, gives the other fellow the first chance at game.

The sportsman doesn't take unfair advantage of another shooter in any way.

Muzzle-loading Rifles

Much of the material in the earlier chapters of this pamphlet applies equally to all riflemen. The material is not repeated in this chapter and should be read by anyone involved in muzzle-loading.

The Background of Muzzle-loading Firearms

Until the introduction of cartridge firearms in the 1800s, most firearms were muzzle-loaded. The firearm came from a discovery more than 500 years ago. It was found that when a highly combustible material was confined and then lighted, the resulting burning or explosion created enough energy to send a projectile over long distances. This was the discovery of the basic firearm design.

The earliest firearms were crude and unpredictable. To the credit of the inventors, many of the major parts developed in the 15th century are still used today. Since their inception, firearms have consisted of three basic parts—the lock (the firing mechanism), the stock (the handle by which the gun is held), and the barrel (the hollow tube through which the projectile travels on its way to the target). These parts are discussed in greater detail later.

The term *muzzle-loader* comes from the fact that all firearms of this variety are loaded through the muzzle.

The evolution of the muzzle-loading rifle spanned a period of four centuries. There are four basic phases of this development.

The Matchlock

The matchlock is one of the earliest forms. The name came from a wicklike piece of material that was lighted before the gun was fired. When the trigger was pulled, the "match" was lowered into a priming pan containing loose black powder.

In ideal conditions, the match ignited the powder. This in turn ignited a charge that had been poured into the barrel through the muzzle. The ignition of the powder forced a ball out of the muzzle with great velocity. Quite frankly, shooters using this kind of firearm may have been excused for keeping their fingers crossed. If it was raining and the priming powder got wet or the lighted wick was put out, the gun wouldn't fire. Weather conditions had to be ideal for a matchlock to operate properly. The first American colonists used matchlocks. Their use continued in Europe until the advent of the flintlock.

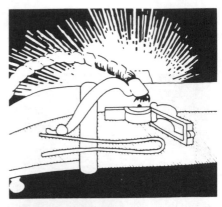

Matchlock action

The Wheel Lock

As technology progressed, gun designers found a way to make firing success less dependent on weather conditions. The successor to the matchlock was the wheel lock. It got its name from a flint and a spinning wheel that made a spark, which caused the powder to ignite. Wheel locks worked a lot like cigarette lighters of today. The shooter used a key that wound a spring-powered steel wheel. When the trigger was pulled, the wheel spun rapidly, creating sparks that ignited the priming powder. The ignited primer then ignited the powder charge in the barrel, firing the shot.

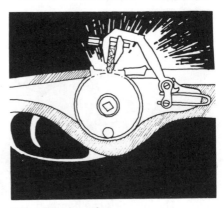

Wheel lock action

Pyrite

The Flintlock

The next major step took place in the late 1600s with the development of the flintlock. With flintlocks, a piece of flint was secured between the jaws

Flintlock action

of the "cock," or hammer as it is commonly called. When the trigger was pulled, the flint struck the frizzen. As the flint contacted the frizzen face, bits of metal were scraped off. These bits of metal were heated by the friction, causing a spark. The frizzen snapped open, exposing the powder in the pan to the cascading sparks, igniting the priming charge in the pan, and causing the main charge in the barrel to fire, projecting the ball out the barrel.

Flint

The Percussion Lock

The final advance in muzzle-loaders took place in the early 1800s. During this era a compound called fulminate of mercury began to replace black powder as a priming agent. This compound was contained in a small metal cup known as a "percussion cap." When the cap was struck by the firearm's hammer, the compound ignited, setting off the powder charge. Percussion caps were the forerunner of the modern cartridge primer.

Cap lock action

Percussion cap

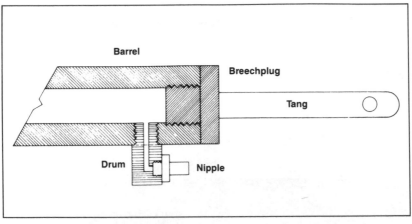

Cutaway of the underside of a typical percussion barrel

Today, the matchlock and the wheel lock are generally found as museum pieces or in the hands of collectors. They are so cumbersome and impractical that few shooters are interested in them beyond their historical value or as collectors' items. Flintlock and percussion muzzle-loaders are alive and well. There are many original muzzle-loading firearms that are still being fired today. The popularity of flintlock and percussion firearms is great enough for manufacturers to make reproductions. These can be found in many sporting goods stores.

Popular models of muzzle-loading rifles are:

Pennsylvania long rifle, a full-stock firearm also known as the Kentucky rifle.

Smoothbore and rifled muskets, both of which are military-style firearms.

Half-stocked mountain rifles, a shorter more easily portable design. The ever-popular Hawken-type rifles are included in this category.

Lock, Stock, and Barrel

You hear this expression frequently. Today it refers to the total of many parts. Actually, it's an old expression. It was used by our forefathers as a means of emphasizing completeness. The fact that the rifle was the source of this description gives you some idea of the importance firearms played in our early history.

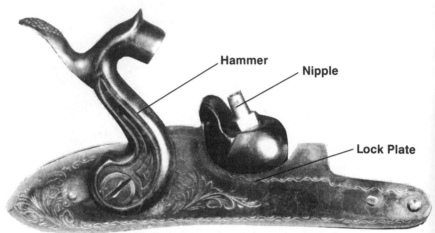

Percussion lock plate, hammer, and nipple

The Lock

The lock of the muzzle-loading rifle is the part that ignites the powder charge, causing the gun to fire. In today's muzzleloading reproductions, the source of ignition depends on whether the gun is a percussion or flintlock model.

In the percussion rifle, ignition is caused by action of the cock, or hammer, striking the percussion cap. The cap contains a combustible priming substance which, when struck and detonated, causes the powder charge to ignite. Pulling the trigger causes the lock to "trip," thus setting off the desired chain reaction necessary for firing.

Practically all replicas are single-trigger copies. With some you first push the trigger forward until a click is heard. This is called a single-set trigger. The trigger is now engaged and can be fired easily with the use of slight finger pressure.

Other muzzle-loaders contain only a simple trigger mechanism. To fire, you must apply full pressure to the trigger.

The Stock

The stock is the handle by which the rifle is held. Stocks come in a variety of shapes and sizes designed to allow secure holding and handling under various shooting conditions.

Each area of the stock has a special name:

- The butt is the part that is placed against the shoulder.

- The wrist is the area where the hand grasps the stock in order to pull the trigger.

- The comb is the top portion of the stock against which the shooter's cheek rests when the gun is held properly.

- The forearm is the front portion of the stock, which extends under the barrel.

The Barrel

The barrel is the hollow metal tube through which the bullet passes when the rifle is fired. Rifle barrels are engineered to stabilize the projectile and ensure maximum accuracy of its path to the target. Three principal terms are associated with the barrel:

- The muzzle is the exit end of the barrel, the portion through which the bullet leaves the gun, and in the case of muzzle-loaders, through which both the powder charge and the bullet are inserted during the loading process.

- The breech is the rear end of the barrel. It is closed by a screwed-in part called the breech plug.

- The bore is the hollow center of the barrel. The diameter of this hole is measured in fractions of an inch or in millimeters. This measurement is called the caliber. A .50 caliber rifle has a bore equal to 50 one-hundredths of an inch, or one-half inch.

Most muzzle-loader barrels have bores with a series of spiral grooves that impart a spiral spin to the bullet as it passes through. This improves the stability of the bullet and promotes accuracy on its way to the target.

The Powder Charge

Black powder was first used around A.D. 1200 as a charge for rock-throwing cannons. It is still essentially unchanged after 800 years. Black powder is a mixture of saltpeter (potassium nitrate), charcoal, and sulfur. It should be noted that over the years several substances have been developed that resemble black powder. Using these with muzzle-loading rifles could be dangerous.

Only commercially manufactured, sporting-grade black powder or Pyrodex offered for sale by a reputable firm should be used in muzzle-loading rifles. The only safe substitute for black powder at present is Pyrodex. It produces nearly identical pressure, bullet velocity, smoke, and noise. It may be used safely as a powder charge in percussion rifles. It is not recommended for use in flintlock rifles because of its difficulty of ignition.

Black powder usable in muzzle-loading rifles will be found in four granulations:

- Fg   Coarse-grain powder used in rifles of .75 caliber or larger.

- FFg   Medium-grain powder used in large rifles (.50–.75 caliber).

- FFFg   Used in small rifles (under .50 caliber), this is the finest-grain black powder safe for use as a powder charge.

- FFFFg   This extra fine-grain powder should be used only for priming flintlocks and never as a main charge.

The finer the powder grain, the quicker it will burn. Rifles with a large bore need slower burning, coarser-grain powder. Smaller-bore rifles need somewhat faster burning powders.

Black powder is classified as an explosive. Certain handling and storage procedures must be observed.

Since it's sensitive to sparks and heat, black powder should be kept in a tightly sealed container. The 1-pound metal container it comes in is ideal. Glass or plastic containers should not be used. The container must be stored away from heat. In some areas, there are local ordinances covering storage procedures for black powder. You should know about any in your area and follow them carefully.

When you pour black powder from its container into a powder horn or flask, you must do so in an open, well-ventilated area. Never use an imitation horn (made of plastic material) to store black powder. Static electricity can be generated and cause ignition. Never permit smoking by anyone near where you are handling black powder. Percussion caps and black powder should be stored separately.

Most muzzle-loading rifles are designed to be used with round, pure lead balls. Others, particularly muskets, use minie-type bullets with a hollow base. Some shooters also use bullet-type projectiles with solid bases.

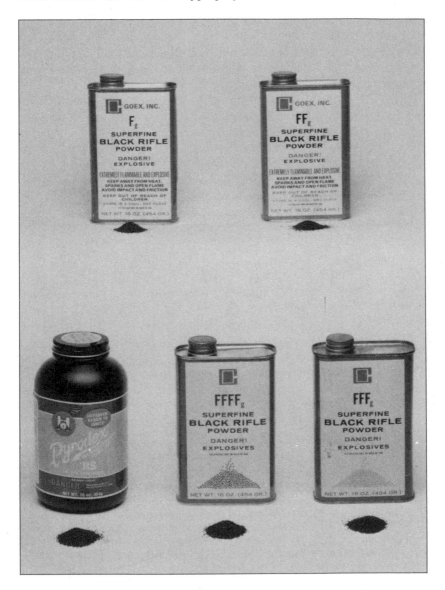

Loading Your Muzzle-loading Rifle

Put a cartridge into the gun's chamber and it's ready to fire. The steps involved in loading a muzzle-loader are much more involved. When you load a muzzle-loader, you'll get the feel of how our ancestors had to function in using the firearms of their day.

You'll need some special equipment and supplies for both loading and cleaning your gun. We'll introduce you to this equipment as we take you through the steps.

Depending on the kind of projectile your rifle is designed to fire, you will find the loading instructions slightly varied. If you're using soft round balls (made of pure lead), it will be necessary to "patch" the ball while loading. Patches aren't needed if your rifle uses hollow or solid-based bullets. The purpose of the patch is to seal the powder gases behind the projectile. It also grips and transfers the spin of the rifling to the ball. The lubrication on the patch helps keep the powder fouling soft.

Items needed for shooting muzzle-loading rifles: (1) Ear protection (muff type), (2) Ear protection (plug type), (3) Eye protection, (4) Possible bag, (5) Patch knife, (6) Patch material, (7) Patch lubricant, (8) Soft lead balls, (9) Ball starter, (10) Powder horn, (11) Powder flask, (12) Priming horn, (13) Percussion caps, (14) Powder measure, (15) Nipple wrench, (16) Nipple pick, (17) Ball puller, (18) Patch puller, (19) Cleaning jag, (20) Loading rod, (21) Cleaning patches, (22) Pregreased patches.

In any case, you will have to use a step-by-step approach, the order of which should never be broken. Basically, the steps involve clearing the barrel, pouring the powder charge, and "seating" the projectile. Since the muzzle-loader is a single-shot firearm, you'll have time to load the same way every time you fire a shot. Before long, the steps will come naturally.

As a beginner, you should have an experienced muzzle-loading shooter with you during your initial loading attempts. An experienced shooter can assist and coach you as you go along. Trying to correct any of the problems you might encounter without the benefit of experienced help could result in a mishap. Always wear eye and ear protection while loading and firing muzzle-loading firearms. **Note: Wear a long-sleeved shirt or jacket made of natural fiber (not synthetic such as nylon) to reduce the chance of injury from flashback.** Use the following steps as a guide for safe and effective handling of your gun.

1. Position the rifle for loading. Stand the rifle on the ground between your legs, with the muzzle pointed up and away from your body. Never work directly over the muzzle. The hammer should be on half cock for a percussion rifle. The flintlock rifle should have the frizzen open with the hammer down during the loading process.

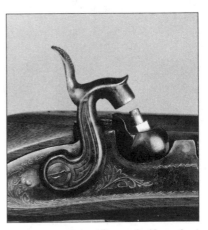

▲ **Percussion rifle on half-cock**

◄ **Position rifle for loading.**

2. Check the bore for load. (See the chapter titled "Gun Safety.") Draw the ramrod out of the stock of your rifle, insert it into the barrel, mark it, and remove the ramrod. Place the ramrod along the outside of the barrel, placing the mark even with the muzzle. The tip of the ramrod should come close to the nipple or flashhole. If after inserting the marked ramrod down the barrel, the mark is above the muzzle level, you may have a gun that's loaded. If you find an indication that there's still a load in the rifle, have an experienced muzzle-loading shooter—or better yet, a qualified muzzle-loading gunsmith—remove the load for you. Never try to clear the load by firing the old charge. You have no way of knowing what has been loaded in the barrel.

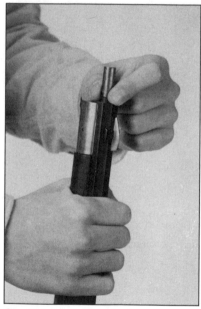

Check bore for load. ▲

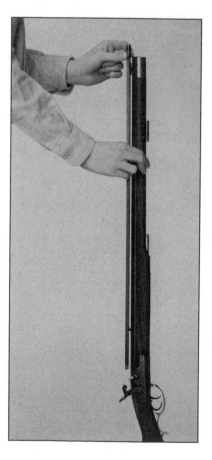

Measure against the ouside of the barrel. ►

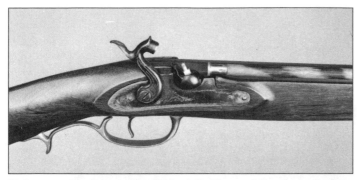

Make sure the ramrod is against the face of the breech plug.

Wipe and clean the barrel.

3. Wipe and clean the barrel. Use your ramrod to run a clean patch up and down the bore. This will remove any excess oil from the bore that might interfere with ignition. If you're using a flintlock rifle, clean and dry the pan area and run a pipe cleaner through the flashhole. With a percussion rifle, dry and clean the flash channel by firing two or three percussion caps on the nipple. Make sure the muzzle is pointed in a safe direction.

When you fire the last of these caps, point the muzzle at a blade of grass or other lightweight object. If the object moves upon firing, you're assured that the channel is open.

4. Measure the powder charge. Never pour powder directly into the barrel from its permanent container. Always use a powder measure. They have been created for this purpose and they allow you to use the correct amount of powder in loading.

Fill your powder measure to the appropriate level from your horn or flask. The manufacturer of your gun can provide guidelines telling you the

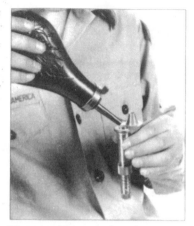

Measure the powder charge. ▲

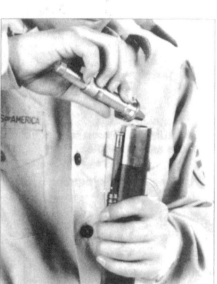

Charge the barrel with powder. ►

powder charge that is recommended for that particular firearm. Never exceed the factory-recommended loading.

Powder charges are measured by weight in grains. A grain equals 1/7000 of a pound. A good rule for starting the load is to provide one grain by weight per caliber. In other words, a .45 caliber rifle would take 45 grains of powder for a starting load. In casual shooting, you may wish to use a little less than the recommended powder charge. This will result in less recoil and noise and will make for a more comfortable and economic shot, with little or no adverse effect on accuracy at close range. Once you've measured the measure from the can, powder horn, or flask, remember to reclose the container. This is standard procedure for black powder handling and an important safety rule.

5. Charge the barrel with powder. Once again with the gun between your legs and the muzzle pointed in a safe direction, use the powder measure to slowly pour powder down the muzzle into the barrel. To make sure that all the powder falls down to the bottom rather than clinging to the side, tap the side of the barrel several times with the heel of your hand.

6. Prepare the patch. As previously mentioned, the use of a patch is required when firing a round ball. If you're using bullets, the next several steps won't be necessary. Patching material must be either 100 percent cotton or linen. Never use a synthetic material, since it may melt in the firing. The first step is lubricating the patch. If you intend to hunt, or are in some other situation where the gun might be loaded for some time without firing, it's best to use some form of commercial patch lubricant, for this purpose.

If, however, you intend to shoot within a few minutes of loading, a "spit patch" lubricated with your own saliva will work nicely. But don't allow a spit patch to stay in your barrel more than a few moments, as it may rust a ring in your bore and cause serious damage to your gun. You can buy precut, prelubricated patches that work well at any time.

7. Patch the ball. Place the lubricated patch squarely over the muzzle of your rifle. Take a single ball and center it directly over the patch. Only a ball made of pure lead is soft enough to enable the patch to impress itself into the ball, thus gripping the ball tightly and imparting the spin of the rifling to the projectile. If you're using a cast or molded lead ball, the slight projection called the sprue (the raised portion of a round ball resulting from the liquid being poured into the mold) must face upward.

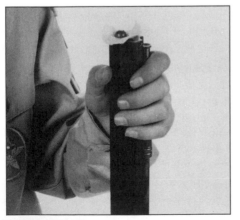

Patch the ball.

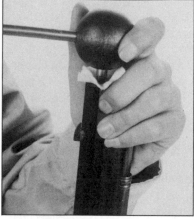

Start the ball and patch. ▲

Trim the patch. ▶

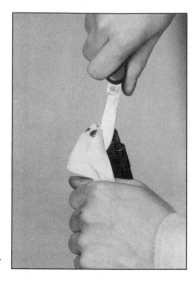

8. "Start" the ball and the patch. You'll need another tool, a starter, to start the ball and patch together and begin driving them through the muzzle. Place the starter over the ball. Strike it with the heel of your hand to drive the ball flush with the muzzle. The force will wrap the cloth around the ball.

9. Trim the patch. If you're using a precut patch, this step shouldn't be necessary. If not, use a patch knife to remove any excess material not wrapped securely around the ball.

10. "Short start" the ball. Once again, take your ball starter. This useful tool includes a shaft that is used to drive the ball deeper into the barrel. This is done by again tapping the starter with the heel of your hand.

"Short start" the ball. ▶

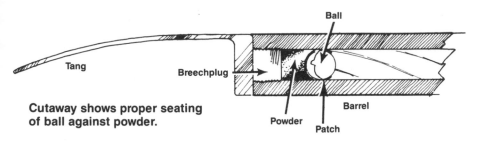

Cutaway shows proper seating
of ball against powder.

11. Seat the ball. Remove the starter, and once again remove the ramrod from the stock. Place the ramrod into the muzzle, holding it no more than 8–10 inches above the muzzle. (Holding it any farther up could result in breaking the ramrod and possibly injuring your hand).

You should encounter only slight resistance in pushing the ball all the way through the barrel. It is vital to ensure that the ball is seated securely against the powder charge. Any gaps between the ball and the powder charge could create a dangerous situation. When you're sure that the ball is tightly against the powder charge, mark your ramrod at the point where it is flush against the muzzle. You will now have two marks on

"Seat" the ball properly.

Marking the ramrod

your ramrod. The first is the mark showing the empty depth of the barrel, and the second shows how far to push the ball to load your rifle securely for subsequent shots.

If for any reason you can't seat the ball all the way down the barrel, the ball will have to be removed and the powder charge cleared. Don't try to do this yourself. Never attempt to fire a load that's not firmly seated.

12. Capping or priming. The last step is priming the flash pan with powder, or placing a percussion cap on the rifle's nipple. Don't attempt to do either of these until you and your gun are at the firing point.

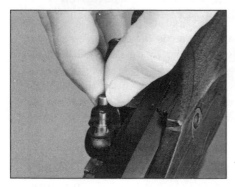

The precise steps to be followed in capping or priming can vary from firearm to firearm. Consult your manufacturer's guidelines to ensure proper use. Be sure the muzzle is pointed in a safe direction when capping or priming.

◄ Capping the cap lock

Failure to Fire

Even if you've followed all the steps carefully, your muzzle-loader could surprise you. There you are, on the range, with your gun carefully aimed. You pull the trigger, and click! The cap fires or the plan flashes and nothing happens.

Several things could have gone wrong. Whatever the case, don't unshoulder your gun immediately. Keep it pointed in a safe direction for a minute or so. There's a very good reason for this. Sometimes a muzzle-loader will not fire immediately when you pull the trigger. It might take a few seconds for the spark to fully ignite the priming or cause the powder to explode. This is called "hang fire." Once you've assured yourself that hang fire will not occur, you can begin troubleshooting.

One of the most common causes of a misfire is a blocked flash channel. It should be the first thing you check for. Run a fine wire through the nipple (on a percussion rifle) or the flash hole (on a flintlock) to make sure the channel is open. Then reprime or recap, and try again.

Still no luck? The problem could be that there's no powder behind the ball. You may have forgotten to put in a powder charge. This is one reason for carefully following the same procedure each time you load. Let nothing distract you when loading. Remember, "First the powder, then the ball, or your gun won't shoot at all." What can be done about this problem?

In a percussion gun, this can be remedied by removing the nipple with a nipple wrench. (Work with your counselor in removing the nipple until you become proficient.) Once the channel is exposed, you can work enough powder behind the ball to enable firing. Reinstall the nipple and recap, then reseat the ball with the ramrod. When you fire this time, the ball will probably be expelled. If not, repeat the whole process, making sure, again, that the ball is reseated. If this will not work, you may need to pull the ball.

Pulling the ball requires two people and a ball-pulling attachment to your ramrod. Attach the ball puller to your ramrod, push it down firmly against the ball, and screw the ball puller into it. Have your partner hold the firearm as you pull the ball from the barrel. Clean the barrel and reload. If the ball cannot be removed in this manner, take the firearm to a competent gunsmith to be removed.

With the flintlock, you can sometimes work enough powder through the flash hole to enable the bullet to be expelled. But that's not always the problem.

Often, a misfire in a flintlock is the result of a dull flint. If the flint isn't sharp enough, the sparks it will send off the frizzen face won't be hot enough to ignite the primer.

To correct this, you'll have to sharpen the flint or put in a new sharp flint. A process called "knapping" is a way of sharpening the flint in the gun, but it's complicated and not for the beginner. It's much simpler just to put in a new flint.

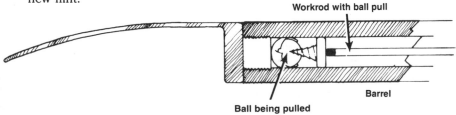

Cutaway shows how a ball puller is used to remove the ball from the barrel.

Keeping It Clean

Each time you fire a muzzle-loading rifle, carbonlike residue is left in the barrel. For this reason, it's best for you to wipe out the barrel each time you fire a shot. After several shots this residue, called "fouling," can become so heavy that the gun will be difficult to load. It can cause a ball to become stuck in the barrel during the loading process. Accuracy is usually better if the bore is wiped between shots.

Wiping is easily done. A cleaning jag of correct size must be attached to the rod. Simply dampen a single cleaning patch—making sure the patch-jag combination is sized properly for a tight fit—and push it down the length of the bore several times. Then duplicate this procedure with a clean, dry patch. Now you're ready for reloading a clean gun. Wiping between shots ensures that no sparks are left glowing in the bore from the previous shot.

Taking Care of Your Gun

A lot of the information in the "Gun Safety" chapter applies to the care of your muzzle-loader. But there are a few differences, and you should note them.

You can protect your rifle by following a basic rule: *Never leave your rifle overnight without a thorough cleaning after shooting.* Generally, a simple solution of hot water and any conventional dishwashing soap and a bottle of cleaning solvent are virtually all you need to keep your gun free of harmful agents. The gun must also be lubricated frequently to protect its moving and stationary metal parts. Commercial black powder solvents are effective in removing residue.

Cleaning the Barrel

Muzzle-loading rifles come in two styles. On one, the barrel can be removed from the standing breech. This is called the hooked breech design. In the second variety, the barrel, breech, and breech plug (or tang) are one piece. The cleaning method will depend on the style of your rifle. Muzzle-loaders with a hooked breech design are cleaned fairly easily:

• Remove the ramrod.

• Bring the hammer to full-cocked position.

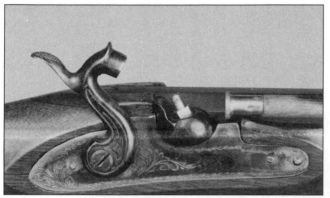

Hammer in full-cocked position

• Remove the nipple if the gun is a percussion firearm.

Remove the nipple.

- Remove the barrel key from the forearm.

Lift the barrel out of the stock.

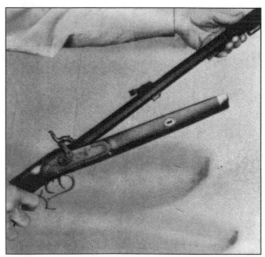

- Take a cleaning rod with a cleaning end or jag attached to its end and fit a soft flannel patch around the jag.

- Saturate the patch with cleaning solvent and wipe the bore several times to loosen the fouling (encrusted buildup from powder) that has accumulated.

- Insert the breech end of the barrel in a bucket of hot, soapy water.

- Stroking the rod in an up-and-down manner, "pump" water from the bucket through the full length of the bore. Repeat several times. Follow the procedure with a bucket of clean, hot water, repeating the pumping action until the barrel is clean.

◄ **Insert the breech end of the barrel in a bucket or container of hot, soapy water.**

Clean the breech, barrel, and tang of your percussion model by using a flush-out nipple.

In cases where the breech, barrel, and tang are all one piece, they must be cleaned together. If your rifle is a percussion model, this can be done by using a flush-out nipple. This part is similar in size and shape to the "shooting nipple" you use with percussion caps. It does have a larger hole for ease in cleaning. To clean:

- After swabbing the bore with a cleaning solvent or liquid soap, remove the shooting nipple and put a flush-out nipple in place.

- Take an 18-inch section of thin plastic or rubber tubing (the kind used as fuel line in model airplanes is ideal) and weight one end.

- Attach the tubing to the flush-out nipple, making sure the fit is tight and snug.

- Insert the weighted end of the tube in a bucket of hot, soapy water so that the water is siphoned through the tube and into the rifle, as the rod is gently moved up and down in the barrel.

- Maintain this action until the gun is thoroughly flushed. Then repeat the procedure with clean, hot water.

While you have the shooting nipple removed, clean it with some soapy water and an old toothbrush or pipe cleaner. Once you've thoroughly cleaned it, blow or wipe it dry, oil lightly, and screw it back in the gun, replacing the flush-out nipple.

If you have a flintlock rifle, you won't be able to use this technique. The one exception is the gun that is equipped with a removable flash hole liner. In this case, the flash hole liner can be replaced with a flush nipple and the above procedure can be followed. In all other cases, you will have to clean the barrel with a series of wet patches, using either hot water or cleaning solution. The flash hole and the rear of the bore may be cleaned with a pipe cleaner.

Drying and Protecting the Barrel

Once you've thoroughly cleaned the barrel, use several clean, dry patches to wipe out the entire length of the bore. Continue to run patches on the inside until they come out clean and dry. Then wipe with an oily patch.

Don't overlook the outside of the barrel. Wipe and inspect all metallic surfaces. Make sure that no moisture has escaped into such hard-to-get places as the breech area and under-rib thimbles.

Cleaning the Lock

Your old toothbrush will come in handy in cleaning the lock. The lock is usually held to the stock by two bolts. It can be removed from the rest of the rifle simply by unscrewing the lock bolts a few turns and tapping the bolt heads gently to loosen the lock plate. Then, unscrew the bolts the rest of the way and carefully remove the lock.

Once the lock is removed, use your old brush to scrub both sides thoroughly. Don't be afraid to use very hot water—the hotter the water, the better the lock will dry. Make sure the mechanism is thoroughly dry. Then, lightly oil both the lock and the lock bolts, and replace the stock.

Cleaning the Stock

The stock on your gun is probably made of a very fine wood. You'll want to keep it free of grime and powder. Remember that powder solvents can hurt a wood finish, so be careful when using them. The stock can be cleaned with water or a commercially manufactured stock finish, using a clean patch or cloth. Once the stock is thoroughly dry, treat it with a light coating of stock oil or wax preservative. Throughout the cleaning process, take extra care to ensure that no water or cleaning fluid is spilled in the space between the stock and the barrel. This moisture, undetected, can cause rust, the unfortunate source of damage to many a cherished firearm.

Boy Scout Standards

Boy Scouts are permitted to fire .22 caliber bolt-action, single-shot rifles, air rifles, shotguns, and muzzle-loading long guns under the direction of a certified instructor, 21 years of age or older, within the standards outlined in current Scouting literature and bulletins. BSA policy does not permit the use of handguns in the Scouting program.

Rifles

The following standards are established for rifles to be used in Boy Scouting:

1. Breech-loading will be single-shot, bolt-action of the .22 caliber rim-fire type only. They may be chambered for the .22 short or .22 long rifle, but not for the .22 WRF (which is a more powerful cartridge). Air rifles are also permitted.

2. Semiautomatic rifles will not be permitted.

3. Repeating rifles having a tubular magazine will not be permitted.

4. Repeating rifles having a removable clip-type magazine will be permitted but must be used as a single-loader.

5. All rifles used must have a trigger pull greater than 3 pounds.

6. Shooting safety glasses and ear protectors are required.

7. All training and shooting activities must be supervised by a currently NRA-certified rifle instructor or coach who is 21 years of age or older.

Muzzle-Loaders

The following standards pertain to use of muzzle-loading long guns in training by members of the BSA:

1. Muzzle-loading rifles must be recently manufactured, percussion only. Recommend .45 or .50 caliber. Rifles made from kits must be checked by an expert gunsmith.

2. Recommended loads of .FFFg blackpowder are not to exceed 1 grain per caliber. One half of this amount is frequently sufficient for target shooting.

3. Shooting safety glasses and ear protectors are required.

4. All training and shooting activities must be supervised by a currently certified NRA or NMLRA muzzle-loading rifle instructor 21 years of age or older.

5. Each Scout must have one instructor or adult coach under instructor supervision when loading or firing.

Books About Rifle Shooting

Bridges, Toby. *Custom Muzzleloading Rifles: An Illustrated Guide to Building or Buying a Handcrafted Muzzleloader.* Stackpole, 1986.

Davis, Henry. *A Forgotten Heritage: The Story of the Early American Rifle.* The Gun Room, 1976.

Grissom, Ken. *Buckskin and Black Powder: A Mountain Man's Guide to Muzzleloading.* New Century, 1983.

Klinger, Bernard, ed. *Rifle Shooting as a Sport.* Barnes, 1981.

O'Connor, Jack. *The Rifle Book.* 3d ed. Knopf, 1978.

Pullman, Bill, and Frank T. Hanenkrat. *Position Rifle Shooting: A How-to Text for Shooters and Coaches.* Winchester Press, 1973.

Magazines

The American Marksman, National Rifle Association of America.

The American Rifleman, National Rifle Association of America.

Acknowledgments

The Boy Scouts of America is grateful to the National Rifle Association for its assistance in developing the revised requirements for the Rifle Shooting merit badge. Much of the material used in this new edition of the *Rifle Shooting* merit badge pamphlet is adapted from the NRA publications *The Basics of Rifle Shooting* and *The Muzzleloading Rifle Handbook* and is used with permission. The Boy Scouts of America is also grateful to Stephen K. Moore for his assistance and review of this publication.